VINTAGE BUTTERFLY JUNK JOURNAL KIT

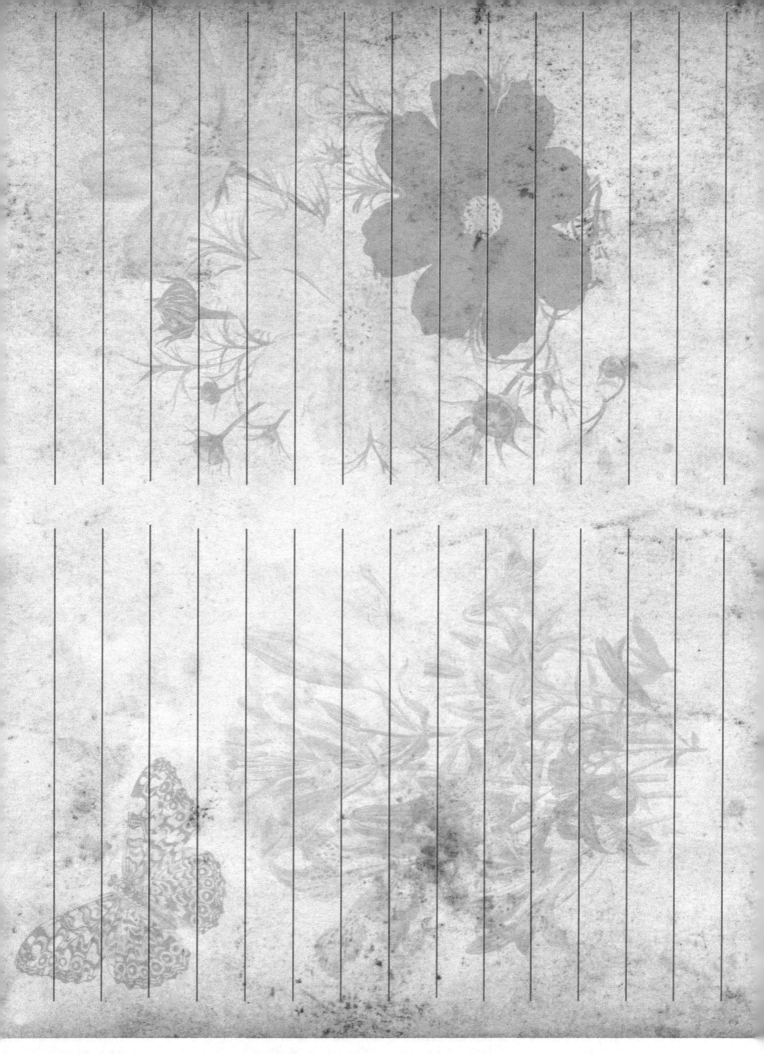

MAULE'S UP TO DATE COLLECTION
OR 8 UNEQUALLED
EVERBLOOMING ROSES.
ONLY 50 CENTS POSTPAID

Wm Henry Maule

ROSES.

DREER'S
Long-spurred Hybrid
AQUILEGIAS
or COLUMBINES

8675309

8675309

4515586

4515586

8675310

8675310

4515587

4515587

8675311

8675311

4515588

4515588

fig. 2.

fig. 4.

1

2

Fig.1.

fig.2.

Fig.3.

3

Blanchard pinx

Fournier sc

B

C

D

Fig 2

669.

B

1a

1

2

Made in United States
Orlando, FL
23 December 2024

56465128R00043